MAYER SMITH

The Disguised Heart of a Heiress

Copyright © 2025 by Mayer Smith

All rights reserved. No part of this publication may be reproduced, stored or transmitted in any form or by any means, electronic, mechanical, photocopying, recording, scanning, or otherwise without written permission from the publisher. It is illegal to copy this book, post it to a website, or distribute it by any other means without permission.

This novel is entirely a work of fiction. The names, characters and incidents portrayed in it are the work of the author's imagination. Any resemblance to actual persons, living or dead, events or localities is entirely coincidental.

Mayer Smith asserts the moral right to be identified as the author of this work.

Mayer Smith has no responsibility for the persistence or accuracy of URLs for external or third-party Internet Websites referred to in this publication and does not guarantee that any content on such Websites is, or will remain, accurate or appropriate.

Designations used by companies to distinguish their products are often claimed as trademarks. All brand names and product names used in this book and on its cover are trade names, service marks, trademarks and registered trademarks of their respective owners. The publishers and the book are not associated with any product or vendor mentioned in this book. None of the companies referenced within the book have endorsed the book.

First edition

*This book was professionally typeset on Reedsy.
Find out more at reedsy.com*

Contents

1	The Heiress Behind the Mask	1
2	A Life of Luxury	7
3	Disappear	13
4	A New Identity	19
5	Unseen Connection	25
6	Meeting	31
7	Fragmented World	38
8	Obsession	45
9	Another Life	52
10	The intimacy	58
11	Fight	65
12	The Watchers	72
13	Falling	79
14	Moments	86
15	Found Love	93

One

The Heiress Behind the Mask

Isabella Hartwell had never been in a room full of strangers. Not in the way she was now. There had always been a few people, a few chosen faces, in every space she occupied. Whether it was at charity galas or exclusive business meetings, there had always been those who knew her, who whispered her name in hushed tones, admiring her elegance, her wealth, her family's legacy. But here, in the dimly lit pub nestled in the corner of a forgotten street, she was just another face in the crowd.

The walls were adorned with chipped wood and faded paintings, the kind of place where time seemed to stand still, and everyone was either lost in their own world or sharing secrets with the bartender. There were no sharp tuxedos or glistening diamonds. The patrons wore faded jeans, leather jackets, and the occasional baseball cap. In this world, Isabella was invisible. It was a strange sensation. And, for once, she didn't mind it.

She adjusted the dark scarf around her neck and tugged the oversized sunglasses farther down her nose. The transformation was startling. No one in this room would recognize her as the heiress to one of the most powerful fortunes in the country, let alone the Hartwell name. She had done her homework, studied the lives of those who lived outside the gilded cage she had been born into. She had perfected the art of blending in, of becoming someone else.

"Is this really necessary?" her best friend, Clara, had asked when Isabella told her of her plans. Clara, ever the skeptic, had watched Isabella with a furrowed brow, her lips pressed into a thin line of concern.

"You don't understand," Isabella had replied, the words almost a whisper. "I need to know if anyone can love me for me. Not for the title, not for the money. Just... for me."

Clara had sighed, throwing her hands up in defeat. "You know you don't have to do this. People love you for who you are, Isabella. Not everyone is just after your money."

But Isabella knew better. The very world she had been born into was built on appearances, on the glint of diamonds and the weight of gold. It was impossible to tell if anyone truly cared about her. Her parents' friends, her "boyfriend" of the past year—none of them had ever truly seen her. She had always been the perfect accessory: poised, graceful, polished. But that wasn't who she was. That wasn't who she wanted to be anymore.

And so, she had done what seemed like the only logical thing: she had disappeared. Gone was the designer wardrobe. Gone was the perfect updo, the manicured nails, the sparkling rings. Isabella Hartwell, the woman everyone thought they knew, was gone. In her place was Lily Williams, a twenty-something woman with tousled brown hair, dressed in a simple black jacket and jeans, her face void of makeup save for a smear of lip balm. She had never felt more liberated. The weight of her past identity had been replaced by the exhilarating freedom of anonymity.

For days, she had wandered the streets of the city, hiding in plain sight. At first, the people she encountered had been indifferent, barely giving her a second glance. But Isabella had taken it all in, basking in the quiet comfort of being just another face in the crowd. She had sat in coffee shops, wandered through parks, and dined in hole-in-the-wall restaurants where no one knew her name. It was liberating. It was terrifying. And it was everything she had ever wanted.

But tonight was different. Tonight, she had made a choice.

Isabella had found herself in this particular pub, standing near the bar, staring at the assortment of drinks as the bartender polished glasses. She hadn't come here for a drink. No, she was here for something else entirely. She had to meet someone. Someone who could look beyond the wealth, beyond the world of privilege that she had been born into. She needed to know that someone could love her for who she truly was.

As the minutes passed, her heart raced. She had come here for a reason. She had come here to meet Ethan.

He had no idea who she was. None. He was a regular at the pub, a quiet man with dark brown eyes and messy hair, always lost in his thoughts as he sipped on his beer or typed away on his laptop. He had never given her a second glance, even when she had walked in that evening. He had no idea that the woman in front of him was Isabella Hartwell—the heiress to a fortune he could never dream of. No one did.

She had met him by accident—or rather, by design. She had carefully watched him from a distance, intrigued by how effortlessly he seemed to blend into the crowd. Unlike the other men she knew, Ethan didn't care about appearances. He didn't flatter her with compliments or try to get closer to her because of her name. He was just… Ethan. And that, to Isabella, was something she hadn't encountered before.

But what if it was all an act? What if he was pretending not to notice her, pretending not to care? What if this was just another facade? What if she couldn't escape the trap of her own life, no matter how hard she tried?

She took a deep breath, steadying her nerves. Her fingers brushed against the edge of her glass. She had spent years in a world of carefully orchestrated interactions. Everything had always been about appearance, about status, about how much people could take from her. But Ethan was different. He didn't seem to want anything from her. There was something genuine about him—a warmth that wasn't tied to her wealth, a kindness that didn't come with strings attached.

At that moment, Ethan looked up, his gaze meeting hers across the room. For a split second, their eyes locked. She quickly looked away, feeling her heart race. Did he recognize her? Did he see through the layers of her disguise? She couldn't know for sure. But she had come this far, and she couldn't turn back now.

"Hey," Ethan's voice was low, carrying a warm lilt. He stepped forward, his eyes studying her with the same quiet curiosity that had intrigued her from the beginning. "You're new around here, aren't you?"

Isabella hesitated before nodding, her pulse pounding in her ears. "I'm just passing through," she said, her voice calm, controlled, but betraying a hint of nervousness.

"Well," Ethan continued with a smile, "in that case, welcome. Can I buy you a drink?"

For the first time in a long while, Isabella didn't feel the need to pretend. She smiled back, her lips curling into a genuine expression that had nothing to do with the public persona she had worn for so long.

"Sure," she said. "I'd like that."

As Ethan turned to order, Isabella took a deep breath, watching the room through a different lens. She was no longer just a heiress in hiding. She was a woman, a real woman, about to discover whether love could be real, too. And for the first time in a long time, she felt hope stirring in her chest. The beginning of something new, something unknown—something she had never dared to imagine before.

For tonight, at least, Isabella Hartwell would cease to exist.

And Lily Williams would see if love could be hers.

Two

A Life of Luxury

The night was growing colder as Isabella (now Lily) stepped outside the pub, the chill of the evening air biting at her skin. She pulled her jacket tighter around her, trying to ward off the emptiness she felt inside. Her brief interaction with Ethan had been unexpected, but not in the way she had hoped. As he'd bought her that drink, as their conversation had flowed effortlessly, there was still a nagging doubt in the back of her mind—what if he knew? What if he could see through the disguise?

It had been easy, slipping into the role of Lily Williams. The name was simple enough, common even, and the appearance she had created for herself—messy hair, plain clothes, and a lack of makeup—seemed to convince everyone around her that she was just another ordinary woman. But tonight, with Ethan, she couldn't shake the feeling that he had noticed something.

Maybe it was the way her eyes sparkled a little too brightly, or the small hesitation in her words when she talked about her past, but the unease lingered. She could tell Ethan was sharp, perceptive in a way that most people weren't.

And yet, when he smiled at her, when he laughed, it all felt so real. For the first time in years, she felt as though someone was truly seeing her. Not the heiress, not the daughter of a legacy, but Lily—a woman who was just trying to exist outside of the life she had been forced to lead.

She took a deep breath, trying to calm the fluttering in her chest. Maybe this was the beginning of what she had been hoping for—a glimpse of something real, something untouched by wealth and status.

But no matter how much she wished to believe it, the shadows of her former life kept creeping back in.

Her phone buzzed in her pocket, the familiar tone sending a jolt of tension through her. She didn't have to look at the screen to know who it was. The number had been programmed into her phone for years, a constant presence she could never escape. She sighed heavily and pulled it out, staring at the screen for a moment before answering.

"Isabella," her father's voice boomed through the phone, deep and commanding. "Where are you?"

Her heart skipped a beat. The voice of her father, a man she had spent most of her life trying to please, trying to escape. "I'm out," she said, her voice steady but edged with the tension she could never quite hide. "I told you, I needed some time."

"Time? You've had plenty of time. Your mother and I have been waiting for you at the estate. We have important guests arriving in the morning, and we expect you to be here. This is no time for your childish games."

Isabella closed her eyes, biting back the anger that threatened to rise in her chest. The pressure, the expectations, they had never stopped. She had always been the perfect daughter, the perfect heiress, groomed to take over the Hartwell empire. But she had never wanted it. She had never wanted a life that was dictated by her family's desires and the endless parade of people who only wanted to be close to her because of her last name.

"I'm not coming home tonight," she said quietly. "I'll be back when I'm ready."

There was a long pause on the other end of the line, and for a moment, Isabella thought her father might hang up. Instead, she heard a sigh, filled with the weight of years of disappointment. "Isabella, don't be foolish. You know your responsibilities. You can't hide away forever."

"I'm not hiding," she replied, her voice firmer now. "I'm just trying to find out who I am without all the noise. Without the… expectations."

"Expectations?" Her father scoffed. "You are the heir to the Hartwell fortune, Isabella. You don't have the luxury of finding yourself. You have a duty to this family."

The words cut deep, but Isabella refused to let them affect her. "I'll be home when I'm ready," she repeated, ending the call before her father could say anything else. She stared at the screen for a moment, her finger hovering over the contacts list as she debated calling Clara. But she quickly dismissed the idea. Clara wouldn't understand. None of her old friends would. No one from her world would understand the suffocating weight of her life.

She slid the phone back into her pocket, trying to shake off the heaviness that lingered. The expectations, the responsibilities—they all seemed so far removed from the life she was building here, in this small corner of the city. The life where she could be someone else. Someone free.

But how long could she keep up the facade? How long could she pretend to be Lily Williams before everything crashed down around her?

She looked back at the pub, where the warm glow of the lights spilled onto the street. Ethan had gone inside to finish his drink, and Isabella had gone home—if only for a moment. She was drawn to the place, to the quiet familiarity of it. There was something about the pub that felt like a refuge, a sanctuary from the world she had abandoned, the world of gold and silver that had always been her prison.

Her thoughts were interrupted by a voice behind her. "Lily?"

She turned around quickly, her heart leaping into her throat, before she saw Ethan standing there, his hands stuffed into the pockets of his jacket. He looked at her with that same warmth in his eyes, his smile genuine.

"You forgot this," he said, holding out her scarf, the one she had left behind in her haste to leave.

For a moment, Isabella was speechless. She hadn't expected him to follow her out. She hadn't expected him to care. She hadn't expected any of this. But there he was, standing before her, his presence grounding her in a way she hadn't felt in years.

"Thank you," she said, her voice soft as she reached out to take the scarf. Their fingers brushed, sending an unexpected spark of electricity through her.

Ethan's eyes lingered on hers for a moment, and she could tell he was searching for something. Was it the same thing she was searching for? A connection? A truth?

"I didn't expect you to leave so soon," he said, his voice casual, but there was a hint of curiosity in his tone. "Did I say something wrong?"

Isabella hesitated, unsure of how to answer. What could she say to him? That she was running from a life that didn't belong to her? That she had no idea what she was doing? That she didn't know how to live without the constant pressure of her family's expectations?

"No," she said finally, her voice steadier than she felt. "It's just… I have a lot on my mind."

Ethan smiled again, a crooked grin that made her heart race. "Well, if you ever feel like talking, I'm here."

Isabella nodded, her throat tight. She couldn't help but wonder how long she could keep this up. How long she could pretend to be someone she wasn't. But in that moment, standing in the cold with Ethan, with his kindness and warmth, she couldn't help but feel a glimmer of hope.

For the first time in a long time, she felt like maybe—just maybe—there was someone who could see beyond the mask. Someone who could see her. Not Isabella Hartwell, but Lily. And maybe, just maybe, she was ready to let him.

Three

Disappear

Isabella sat in her luxury penthouse, staring out at the shimmering skyline of the city. The lights below twinkled like stars, each one a reminder of the life she was bound to. The floor-to-ceiling windows framed the bustling city, and yet, in the solitude of her high-rise, she felt more isolated than ever. She had lived in this world all her life—an oasis of privilege, a kingdom of wealth where she was both revered and imprisoned. But as she watched the cars move like ants below, a sharp realization cut through her: she was invisible in her own life.

The soft hum of the city below couldn't drown the voices in her mind, the voices of expectations that had grown louder and more suffocating with every passing year. Her father's booming command, her mother's polite, but constant reminders of her duties, the board meetings, the endless charity events, the photographers who snapped her every move—it was all too much. She had long stopped being Isabella Hartwell, the woman she was born to be. Now, she was just a symbol, an heir to a fortune, a trophy in a world where appearances mattered more than substance.

And there, in the midst of her golden cage, was the truth she had buried for so long: she was lonely. No, not just lonely—she was drowning. In her endless sea of wealth, power, and recognition, she had lost herself. She couldn't remember the last time anyone had looked at her and seen her—the person behind the diamond-studded mask. The person with fears, desires, dreams, and doubts.

Her gaze shifted to the photo on her desk. A picture of her family—her mother with her polished smile, her father's stern eyes, and herself standing in the middle, always smiling, always poised. It was the perfect picture of the perfect family. The kind of image that belonged in a magazine, in a storybook. But behind the smiles were secrets, behind the wealth were sacrifices, and behind the perfect life was a woman who didn't know who she was anymore.

And that woman, Isabella Hartwell, had had enough.

The night before had been a turning point. Ethan's presence at the pub had struck something deep inside her. The way he had treated her—so genuinely, so simply—was like a breath of fresh air. He had no idea who she really was, no idea about her wealth, her last name, or the world she came from. He saw her as a woman. As Lily. He didn't want anything from her—no business deals, no status boost, no entry into her world. He wanted nothing more than a conversation, a drink, a laugh.

But the guilt gnawed at her. What would happen if he found out who she really was? Would he think she was using him? Would he feel betrayed? Could their connection survive the truth? Could she survive it?

Her phone buzzed on the desk, and she glanced at the screen, the familiar number lighting up her display. It was her father. She quickly pressed the button to decline the call. It wasn't that she didn't love her parents, but she couldn't keep up with the weight of their expectations anymore. They wanted her to marry into one of the oldest families in the country, to make business connections, to carry on the Hartwell legacy. They had chosen a suitor for her years ago—David Wellington, a man who was just as wealthy and powerful as her family, a man who would be an asset to the family business.

But David didn't see her. He saw the heir, the title, the fortune. The marriage was a business transaction, not a union of two people who loved each other. She had never felt the slightest connection to him, never once looked into his eyes and felt anything other than duty. And now, with each passing day, her parents pressed harder, as if the weight of their desires was something she could simply bear without breaking.

Isabella stood from her desk, her fingers brushing the edge of the glass that separated her from the world below. The city sprawled beneath her, a mirror of her own world—beautiful, intricate, and cold. But she couldn't take it anymore. Not the expectations. Not the loneliness. Not the suffocating roles that had been assigned to her.

She needed to disappear.

It wasn't just a desire anymore. It was a need. A deep, unrelenting craving to shed her skin and step into a life where no one knew her, where no one cared about her last name or her bank account. A life where she could be free of the constant pressure to conform to a mold that wasn't hers to begin with. A life where she could discover who she really was, without the layers of wealth and power smothering her every move.

But disappearing was a dangerous game. It wasn't just a matter of walking away from her penthouse and leaving the city behind. She would have to erase every trace of herself. Her family's security team would be on alert. Her private planes, her driver, her personal assistant—everything in her world was designed to keep her tethered to a life she could no longer bear. Even her digital footprint was meticulously monitored, her movements tracked, and her interactions analyzed.

She couldn't just vanish. She needed a plan, a strategy that would allow her to slip away without a trace. She had to be clever. She had to be methodical.

Her first step was to sever her connections. She couldn't afford to keep up appearances, couldn't afford to leave a trail behind her. That meant saying goodbye to Clara, her only real friend, the one person who had always been there for her. Clara would never understand, but she would have to accept it. There would be no farewell parties, no final hugs. Isabella Hartwell had to disappear, and in order to do so, she would have to sever every tie to the life she had known.

She walked to her bedroom and opened the closet door. Rows of designer dresses, shoes, and accessories filled the space—each item a symbol of the life she was leaving behind. The luxury, the perfection—it all seemed so empty now. With trembling fingers, she picked out a simple black jacket and a pair of faded jeans. Nothing too flashy. Nothing too memorable. She would have to blend in, to become someone who didn't stand out, someone who could disappear into the crowd.

Next, she turned to her phone. It was her lifeline, the connection to her family, to her life. She scrolled through the contacts list, each name a reminder of the life she was leaving behind. Her parents, her business associates, the friends who had never truly been her friends—she deleted them all. Each name vanished with a click, each number lost to the void. It felt freeing, like peeling off the last layer of armor she had worn for so long.

The hardest part was her parents. She had never disobeyed them before, never even entertained the thought of going against their wishes. But now, in this moment of raw clarity, she knew what she had to do. She had to cut all ties, even with the people who had given her life. She typed out a message to her mother, one that would have to be enough. She didn't have the strength to speak it aloud.

"I need some time to myself. I need to figure out who I am. I'll be back when I'm ready."

The words felt hollow, but they were the only ones she could offer. She pressed send, her heart racing as she wondered what the consequences would be. Would her mother try to track her down? Would her father send people to bring her back? She didn't know, but she couldn't worry about that now. Disappearing meant taking risks. It meant being willing to lose everything for a chance at freedom.

Isabella stood in the center of her room, the weight of her decision crashing over her. She was about to walk away from everything she had known—her family, her fortune, her legacy. But in that moment, as she took a deep breath, she realized something: for the first time in her life, she was finally in control. And for the first time in years, she felt alive.

With one final glance at the life she was leaving behind, she turned and walked out the door.

Four

A New Identity

The rain came down in sheets, the city streets transformed into a blur of puddles and reflections. Isabella, now Lily Williams, walked briskly down the dimly lit alley, her heart pounding in her chest. She had done it. She had finally done it. She had walked away from her old life, severed all ties, and stepped into the unknown.

She could hear the pounding of her boots against the wet pavement, each step a reminder that she was moving further and further away from the woman she used to be. The last few hours had been a whirlwind of decisions, packing a few essentials, deleting her contacts, erasing her existence from the world she once ruled. She had left her penthouse, her family, her life behind. There would be no more grand parties, no more corporate meetings, no more scrutinizing eyes watching her every move. She was free, and the realization of that freedom made her skin tingle with a mixture of fear and excitement.

The dim lights of the city flickered overhead as she ducked into a small, inconspicuous building—an old apartment complex on the edge of town, far from the hustle and bustle of her old world. It wasn't glamorous or luxurious. The walls were peeling, and the floors creaked under her weight. But it was perfect. Here, she could disappear.

Isabella, now Lily, took a deep breath as she fumbled for the key she had picked up earlier from the landlord. She had been careful in choosing this place—far enough from her family's network of spies, far enough from any prying eyes that might recognize her. She had traded her silk gowns for faded jeans and oversized jackets. She had abandoned her diamond earrings for a simple silver chain that barely caught the light. This was her new life now, and it was as far removed from the woman she had been as possible.

Inside, the apartment was bare, with only the most basic furnishings—a worn-out couch, a small coffee table, and a bed with a threadbare blanket. The windows were covered with cheap curtains, and the air smelled faintly of mildew. It was nothing like the penthouse she had left behind. It was nothing like the world she had come from. But it was real. It was raw. And for the first time in her life, it felt like home.

She set down her small bag on the coffee table, glancing around the room as if expecting it to speak to her. But there was nothing—no lavish decorations, no family portraits, no reminders of her old life. Just a small, quiet space where she could finally begin to understand who she really was.

Lily ran her fingers through her messy hair, feeling the unfamiliar weight of it. The long locks she used to carefully maintain had now been allowed to fall into natural waves. No more stylists, no more manicures. She was no longer Isabella Hartwell, the heiress. She was Lily Williams, an ordinary woman with a blank slate.

She stood there for a long moment, the silence of the apartment overwhelming her senses. She had imagined this moment for years, dreamt of what it would feel like to break free from the suffocating life she had been born into. But now that she was free, now that she had taken the first step into the unknown, the reality of it was heavier than she had expected. She had no plan, no direction. She had no idea what she was supposed to do now.

With a sigh, she moved to the small kitchen in the corner of the room, rummaging through the cupboards for something to eat. She had already spent too much time thinking, overthinking, and now she needed something to ground her. A meal. A simple act of survival. She found a can of soup, heated it up, and sat at the small table, staring at the steam rising from the bowl.

It wasn't glamorous, but it was hers.

The phone in her pocket buzzed, breaking the silence. She hesitated for a moment before pulling it out, her stomach knotting in anticipation. It was an unknown number. For a moment, she considered ignoring it. But her curiosity got the better of her. She swiped to answer.

"Hello?" Her voice sounded foreign, even to herself.

"Isabella?" The voice on the other end was sharp, authoritative. Her father.

She froze. The sound of his voice, even after everything she had done to cut ties, still held a power over her. She felt the old pang of guilt rise in her chest. She had hoped that once she disappeared, she would be free from his demands, his expectations. But it seemed he wasn't so easily fooled.

"Isabella, where are you?" Her father's voice was demanding, the way it always was when he wanted something.

She glanced around the small apartment, her breath catching in her throat. The apartment that had no connection to the world she had left behind, the world where she had been forced to play a role. "I… I'm not coming back, Dad," she said, her voice steady despite the tremor in her chest. "I need some time. I need to figure things out."

There was a pause on the other end of the line. She could almost hear her father's mind working, his frustration building. "You're making a mistake, Isabella. You can't just walk away from everything we've built. You have a duty to this family, to the company."

"I don't care about the company," she said, the words slipping out before she could stop them. It was the truth—she had never

A New Identity

cared about the company, the business empire her father had built. It had always been about control, about power, about what was expected of her. But none of that mattered anymore.

"You don't understand," her father replied, his voice cold. "You are the future of the Hartwell legacy. You can't just… disappear."

"I can, Dad," she said, her voice firm now. "I'm done with it all. I'm done with being Isabella Hartwell."

The line went dead.

Lily stared at the phone in her hand, her heart racing. She had done it. She had finally said it. She had finally broken free. But even as the words left her mouth, a part of her—the part that had been raised to always please, to never disappoint—began to panic. What had she just done? How far would her father go to drag her back into his world? How far would her mother go to ensure she didn't stray too far from the path they had set for her?

She shook her head, pushing the thoughts aside. This was what she wanted. She had made the choice, and there was no going back now.

Lily set the phone down, her fingers trembling as she tried to steady herself. She had no plan, no resources, no allies in this new life. But she had something far more valuable: freedom. The freedom to be who she wanted to be. To live a life that wasn't dictated by the weight of her family's legacy. To experience the world on her own terms.

She stood up from the table, moving toward the window and staring out at the city below. It was a small apartment, far from the opulence she had known. But for the first time in her life, it felt like enough.

As the rain continued to pour outside, Lily knew that her journey was just beginning. She didn't know what the future held or how long she could keep up this charade. But for now, she was free. Free to build a new life, free to find herself. And that, she realized, was all that mattered.

For the first time in years, Lily Williams didn't feel alone.

She felt alive.

Five

Unseen Connection

The city was alive in the hours after midnight, its pulse quickening with the neon lights and the hum of distant traffic. The streets, once bustling with the frenzy of the day, now seemed quiet, almost peaceful, under the cloak of darkness. But for Lily, standing in front of her small apartment's window, it felt like everything was moving too fast. She had come so far, yet the distance between her old life and this new existence felt insurmountable.

Lily glanced at her reflection in the glass. Her eyes were wide, haunted, as though the weight of the decision she had made still hadn't fully settled in her chest. The rain had stopped, leaving the streets below glistening like dark mirrors, reflecting the glow of the streetlights. It was a quiet night, one that almost begged for introspection, but Lily had learned long ago to ignore the voice in her head that whispered doubts and fears.

She turned away from the window, wiping her hands on the jeans she had worn for days. The decision to leave everything behind was final, and yet, each passing moment felt like a test of her resolve. The phone call with her father had rattled her more than she cared to admit. His voice, so authoritative, so filled with expectation, echoed in her ears long after she had ended the conversation. She had never dared to defy him before. Never even considered it. But now, she was doing it. She was defying everything she had known, and she couldn't help but wonder: Was she truly free, or had she simply run away?

A knock at the door interrupted her thoughts. It was sharp, deliberate—a sound that was too urgent to be ignored.

Her heart skipped a beat. She hadn't expected anyone. She hadn't told anyone where she was. She quickly moved to the door, her breath catching in her throat as she pressed her ear against the wood. Who could it be? Had someone from her old life found her? Her father's people? Had Clara somehow tracked her down?

She took a step back, her fingers gripping the doorknob with a tension she couldn't shake. She had to be careful. She couldn't risk being found. She had chosen this life. She had to live it. No matter the cost.

The knock came again, louder this time, almost impatient.

Lily took a deep breath, letting it out slowly. She was being paranoid. It was probably just a neighbor, someone who had heard the rain and thought she needed help. She steadied herself and opened the door.

Standing there, in the dim light of the hallway, was Ethan.

His dark eyes met hers with a warmth that made her heart skip. He looked different in the early morning light, his usual confident demeanor replaced by something softer, something unsure. He was holding a bag, the strap slung over his shoulder, and the slight rain that had started up again clung to his jacket. He looked out of place in this building, in this part of the city, as though he didn't belong in the world she was trying to escape.

For a moment, neither of them spoke. Lily stood there, frozen, caught between the fear of being discovered and the inexplicable pull she felt toward him. He had no idea who she really was. He had no idea what she had left behind. But the way he was looking at her now—so patiently, so expectantly—made her wonder if he was somehow beginning to see through the layers of her disguise.

"What are you doing here?" she asked, her voice quieter than she intended. She didn't want him to see the vulnerability in her eyes, the uncertainty that seemed to rise up whenever he was near.

Ethan smiled, a small, almost apologetic curve of his lips. "I know it's late. I was thinking about you, actually." He stepped closer, and Lily instinctively took a step back, feeling the cool wall behind her. "I wasn't sure if you'd be here, but I couldn't stop thinking about our conversation last night. You were… different. Like there was more you weren't saying. And I wanted to check on you."

Lily's breath caught in her throat. How could he have noticed? How could he have known that behind the casual conversation, behind the laughter, she was hiding something so deep, so real?

"Why would you do that?" she asked, her voice barely above a whisper. She hated how weak she sounded, how unsure she felt. He was a stranger. He had no right to care about her, not in the way he did. But then again, she wasn't a stranger to him anymore. She wasn't sure what she was to him.

"I don't know," Ethan said, his voice low and serious now. "I guess... I guess I just wanted to make sure you were okay. You seemed like you needed someone to talk to. And, if I'm being honest, I didn't want to leave things hanging between us."

The sincerity in his voice hit her like a physical blow. She had no idea how to respond. How could she tell him that she wasn't the woman he thought she was? That she wasn't just Lily Williams, the waitress at a small café? How could she tell him that she had stepped into this new life with the hope that maybe, just maybe, someone would love her for who she really was—and now, here he was, reaching out to her, caring about her in a way that terrified her?

"Ethan, I—" she began, but her words faltered. She didn't know what to say. How could she explain herself without revealing everything? How could she tell him that she was running from a life that no longer fit her? That the person he was starting to see was not the person she had always been, but someone entirely new?

Ethan stepped forward, the gap between them closing. His gaze softened as he looked at her, almost as though he could read her mind. "You don't have to explain anything," he said, his voice quiet but firm. "I just... I just wanted to make sure you knew you weren't alone."

And in that moment, something inside of her shifted. The walls she had built around herself, the ones she had spent so long constructing, began to crack. He was here, standing in front of her, offering something she had never asked for but desperately needed—connection. Not the kind of connection that came with expectations or obligations, but something raw, something real.

Lily's breath caught in her throat. "Why are you doing this?" she asked, her voice barely a whisper.

Ethan paused, as if the question had caught him off guard. "Because I think... I think we're connected, Lily. And I don't know what this is or where it's going, but I feel like we have something. I don't know if you feel it too, but I had to come here tonight. I had to know."

Lily felt the weight of his words settle over her, heavy and full of meaning. She had never allowed herself to feel this vulnerable, this exposed. She had always hidden behind the walls of her wealth, her privilege, her mask. But in Ethan's presence, those walls began to crumble. She didn't know how to handle it, didn't know what to say.

For a long moment, there was only the sound of their breathing, the quiet tension that hung between them like an unspoken promise. Lily felt the pull in her chest, the undeniable connection between them that she couldn't explain. And for the first time in a long time, she wanted to believe it. She wanted to believe that maybe, just maybe, Ethan saw her as something more than the woman she had been pretending to be. Maybe he saw her for who she truly was.

"I'm not who you think I am," Lily said finally, her voice trembling with the weight of the truth she had been hiding.

Ethan's eyes softened. "I don't care who you were. I care about who you are now."

Lily's breath caught in her throat as she looked into his eyes, seeing the sincerity, the kindness, the quiet strength. And in that moment, as the world seemed to hold its breath, she felt an unfamiliar warmth spreading through her—a feeling she had long forgotten. For the first time since she had disappeared, she didn't feel alone. She didn't feel invisible.

Maybe, just maybe, there was hope for her in this new life.

And maybe, just maybe, Ethan was the key to finding out who she was really meant to be.

Six

Meeting

Lily sat on the edge of the bed, her knees pulled up to her chest, eyes locked on the door. The words Ethan had spoken the night before hung in the air, suspended between them, like a breath that neither dared to exhale too soon. They had parted ways on a note of uncertainty—something in Ethan's eyes that made her heart ache with an emotion she couldn't quite place, and her own admission that she wasn't who she seemed. It had felt like the beginning of something. But what?

As the days went by, a heavy silence settled over her apartment. Ethan didn't call. He didn't show up at the café where she worked. It was as if he had vanished, leaving nothing behind but the memory of his warm eyes and the quiet promise in his voice. The connection had felt so real, so genuine in that moment. But now, with each passing day, Lily felt the familiar sting of loneliness creeping back in, that ever-present shadow that had followed her for years.

She stared at her reflection in the small, cracked mirror above the dresser, her thoughts racing. What had she expected, anyway? A sudden breakthrough? A miraculous moment where everything about her past life would be forgotten, where Ethan would be the one person to understand her need for freedom, her desire to be loved for who she truly was?

Maybe she had been foolish. Maybe she had imagined that a stranger, someone completely outside her world, could offer her the kind of understanding she had longed for. But who was she kidding? How could someone like Ethan ever understand a woman like her?

Her mind began to drift, slipping back into the labyrinth of memories she had fought so hard to escape. The bustling halls of her family's mansion. Her mother's polished smile. The endless meetings and charity galas. The whispers of her father's colleagues as they discussed everything from mergers to investments to her future, as if she were no more than a piece in a carefully orchestrated puzzle.

She closed her eyes, pushing those thoughts away. She couldn't afford to go back there—not when everything she had worked for, everything she had risked, was on the line.

The knock at the door startled her, making her heart leap into her throat. She stood up quickly, her hands trembling slightly as she moved across the room. Could it be him? Could it really

Meeting

be Ethan?

She opened the door, only to find a woman standing there instead. Her long, dark hair framed her sharp features, her eyes scanning Lily with an intensity that made her feel like an intruder in her own space.

"Lily Williams?" the woman asked, her voice smooth but edged with a hint of authority.

Lily blinked, caught off guard. "Yes, that's me," she replied, her voice tight.

The woman studied her for a moment, as though weighing something in her mind. Then, without saying another word, she stepped forward, brushing past Lily and into the apartment. She moved with a quiet grace, as if she had done this a thousand times before.

Lily stood frozen in the doorway, confused and wary. "Who are you?"

The woman turned, giving her a small, almost polite smile. "I'm here to help," she said simply. "I'm not here to hurt you, if that's what you're worried about."

"Help?" Lily repeated, her heart hammering. "Help with what?"

The woman didn't answer immediately. Instead, she moved to the window and pulled the curtains aside, looking out over the city. She glanced back at Lily, her expression unreadable.

"You don't know it yet, but your life is about to change," she said cryptically.

Lily frowned, feeling a chill creep down her spine. "I don't understand. What do you want from me?"

The woman's eyes softened slightly. "My name is Amelia," she said, her voice steady. "And I've been following you for a while now."

Lily's breath caught in her throat. "Following me?" she repeated, her mind racing. "Why?"

Amelia turned back toward her, her gaze sharp but not unkind. "Because I know who you really are, Lily. I know what you've been running from, and I know why you've disappeared."

Lily took a step back, panic rising in her chest. "I don't know what you're talking about."

Amelia smiled, almost as if she had expected this reaction. "You can't outrun the truth forever. The truth has a way of finding you, no matter how far you go or how carefully you hide."

Lily's hands clenched into fists at her sides. "I don't know who you are, and I don't want anything to do with you," she said, her voice firm but trembling. "You need to leave."

Amelia didn't move, her gaze never wavering. "I can't leave. Not yet. Because you're not the only one in danger, Lily. You're not the only one being watched."

Meeting

The words hit her like a physical blow. "Watched?" Lily echoed, her pulse racing. "What are you talking about?"

"Your family isn't the only one with eyes on you," Amelia said, her voice lowering. "There are people looking for you—people who don't care about your well-being, people who have far more power than you can imagine. And they won't stop until they find you."

Lily's chest tightened. She felt the walls of her small apartment closing in around her. "What do you want from me?" she whispered.

"I want to help you," Amelia replied, her tone gentle now. "I want to help you before it's too late."

Lily was shaking now, her mind spinning with a thousand thoughts. She had left everything behind to escape the life her family had built for her, to find something real—something that wasn't tainted by expectations or manipulation. But now, in the span of a few minutes, her entire world had turned upside down. The woman standing in front of her knew things about her that no one else could possibly know. She knew what Lily had tried so desperately to leave behind.

"I can't trust you," Lily said, her voice low but resolute. "You don't know anything about me. You don't know what I've been through."

"I don't need to know everything," Amelia said softly. "I know enough to know that you're in danger, and I know enough to know that you're not going to survive this alone."

The words rang in Lily's ears, heavy with the weight of the reality she hadn't wanted to face. She had tried to bury her past, to start over, but Amelia's presence in her life was a stark reminder that the past was never truly gone. It lingered, like a shadow, ready to swallow her whole.

"Why are you telling me this?" Lily asked, her voice barely above a whisper.

Amelia took a step toward her. "Because you're not the only one who's been watched. Ethan has been too."

Lily's heart stopped. "Ethan?" she repeated, her voice cracking. "What do you mean?"

"Ethan is more involved in this than you think," Amelia said, her eyes locked on Lily's. "He's been unknowingly dragged into your world, and the people watching you… they're watching him too."

The words were a blur in Lily's mind, her thoughts racing as she tried to make sense of it all. Ethan. He had been so kind to her. So real. But now she realized that her connection with him had never been just about the two of them. It had always been about something bigger. Something far darker.

"You need to trust me," Amelia said, her voice low but insistent. "You need to come with me. Before it's too late for both of you."

Meeting

Lily's breath caught in her throat as the weight of Amelia's words settled over her. She had been running from the truth, from the life she had left behind. But now, standing in front of this mysterious woman, she realized that running might not be enough. The truth was coming for her—faster than she could outrun it.

And as much as it terrified her, she knew one thing for certain: she couldn't do this alone.

Not anymore.

"I'll go with you," Lily said, her voice trembling, but firm. "But I need to see Ethan. I need to know he's okay."

Amelia nodded, her gaze unwavering. "We'll make sure he's safe. But we don't have much time."

As they left the apartment together, the silence that surrounded them was filled with the weight of everything that had led Lily to this moment. Her life was no longer her own. And the path ahead was uncertain, but one thing was clear: nothing would ever be the same again.

Seven

Fragmented World

Lily's heart thudded in her chest as she followed Amelia down the narrow hallway of the apartment building, the sound of their footsteps echoing in the quiet, dimly lit space. The walls were cracked and stained, the air thick with the scent of stale cigarettes and cleaning chemicals that never quite masked the building's age. It was a far cry from the pristine, polished world she had left behind—the world of glass towers, designer everything, and the hollow comfort of privilege. Now, in this strange new reality, every step she took felt like a leap into the unknown.

Amelia led the way, her stride confident and purposeful, as if she had been navigating the shadows of the city for years. She barely glanced over her shoulder to see if Lily was keeping up, but Lily had no choice but to follow. Her mind was reeling with a thousand questions, each one more urgent than the last. What did Amelia know about Ethan? What did she mean when she said Ethan had been "dragged into" Lily's world? How was it possible for something so simple, something so real, to become entangled with the dangers lurking just beneath the surface of her life?

The air outside was heavy with the promise of rain, a thick blanket of clouds pressing down on the city. The streets were wet from the previous downpour, puddles reflecting the faint glow of the streetlights. As they walked, the rhythm of their footsteps fell into sync, the only sound between them. Lily glanced at Amelia, her brow furrowed with suspicion, her thoughts racing.

"What's really going on?" Lily asked, her voice low but insistent. "Why are you here? Why are you telling me all of this?"

Amelia didn't answer immediately. She turned a corner, heading toward a nondescript black sedan parked against the curb. The headlights were off, and the car looked out of place in the otherwise quiet neighborhood. The darkened windows gave it an air of mystery, a silent warning that whoever was inside wasn't someone you wanted to meet.

When they reached the car, Amelia stopped and turned to face Lily. Her eyes were darker now, more serious than they had been back in the apartment. "This isn't just about you anymore, Lily. This is bigger than anything you've imagined. Ethan is involved because of his connection to you—his proximity to you, to your past. And there are people who will stop at nothing to make sure that connection is severed."

Lily's stomach churned. "Who are these people? What do they want with us?" Her mind raced, jumping from one possibility to another, but none of them felt right. This wasn't some typical story. This was her life now, a life she hadn't chosen but had been thrust into with every step she took.

Amelia didn't answer immediately. Instead, she opened the door to the sedan, gesturing for Lily to get inside. "You're not going to like what I have to say next," she said softly. "But you need to hear it if you're going to survive."

Lily hesitated, her body stiff with apprehension. She had no choice. She had already crossed this line. She couldn't turn back now. Taking a deep breath, she slid into the back seat, the cold leather of the seat making her shiver as the door shut behind her. She glanced out of the window, the city lights blurring as the car pulled away from the curb and into the darkened streets.

The drive was long, the silence between them heavy and unyielding. As the car navigated through the twisting streets of the city, Lily's mind raced with images of Ethan. She couldn't shake the memory of the way he had looked at her, the way his presence had grounded her, made her feel as if there was someone out there who saw her, who understood her. And now, the uncertainty of his safety gnawed at her. What had she gotten him into? What had she brought into his life?

Finally, after what felt like an eternity, the car slowed, and Amelia spoke again, her voice breaking the silence. "We're almost there. When we get inside, you need to stay close. Don't say anything about your past. Don't mention your real name.

Just… stay quiet and let me do the talking."

Lily swallowed hard, the knot in her stomach tightening. She didn't ask any more questions. Amelia had already made it clear that she was in the dark about more than just the immediate danger. There were layers to this world—layers Lily had never known, layers that she didn't want to know. But it was too late for ignorance. She was already tangled up in it.

The car came to a stop in front of an unassuming building in a darkened part of town. It was an older building, a relic from another era, its stone exterior cracked and worn with age. There were no signs, no markings to indicate what was inside, just a steel door with a small, inconspicuous keypad next to it. Amelia didn't hesitate. She typed in a code, and the door clicked open.

Lily followed her inside, the cool air of the building cutting through the heat of her anxiety. The hallway was dimly lit, the walls lined with outdated posters, flickering lights casting strange shadows on the floor. The deeper they went into the building, the more the air seemed to thicken with tension, a strange hum vibrating in the silence.

"Stay close," Amelia repeated, her voice a sharp whisper as they reached the door at the end of the hallway. She knocked twice, then once more, her eyes scanning the area around them.

The door opened just a crack, and a pair of eyes appeared through the narrow slit. The door swung open fully, revealing a man standing inside, his posture rigid, his face unreadable.

"Amelia," he said in a low voice, his eyes flicking briefly to Lily before returning to Amelia. "Everything's in place."

Amelia nodded, and they both stepped inside. The room was small but functional, dimly lit with a few old chairs and a table cluttered with papers and half-empty mugs. A tall man stood at the far side of the room, his arms crossed, watching them with an intensity that made Lily's heart skip a beat. His gaze lingered on her for a moment, a flicker of recognition in his eyes before he nodded in greeting.

"This is Lily," Amelia said, her voice calm but firm. "She's the one we've been talking about."

The man's expression shifted slightly, his lips tightening as he took in Lily's appearance. "So, it's true," he murmured. "She's the one."

Lily looked from the man to Amelia, confusion and fear swirling in her chest. "What is this place? What's going on? And who are you people?"

The man didn't answer right away. Instead, he stepped forward, his eyes never leaving her face. "You're more important than you realize, Lily," he said, his voice low and steady. "And you're in far more danger than you know."

The words hung in the air, thick with gravity. Lily's pulse raced, a sudden wave of panic flooding her system. She had known, deep down, that her past would catch up to her eventually. But she hadn't expected this. She hadn't expected the tension, the shadows, the looming threat that seemed to stretch far beyond the edges of her comprehension.

"The people who are after you," the man continued, his voice cutting through her thoughts, "they're not just interested in your family's wealth. They're interested in something much more dangerous—something that, if left unchecked, could tear apart everything you've ever known. And Ethan…"

Lily's breath caught. "Ethan?" she whispered, her mind spinning. "What does he have to do with this?"

The man's gaze softened slightly. "He's more involved than either of you realize. But don't worry. We're going to protect him. We're going to protect you both. But you need to understand one thing." He paused, his eyes locking with hers, his voice dropping to a near whisper. "You're not just running from your past anymore. You're running from a war."

Lily's world tilted. Everything she had known, everything she thought she understood about her life, had just shattered in an instant. A war. A war that had been waging in the shadows for years, and she—she was the reason it had all come to the surface.

As the man's words sank in, Lily realized something terrifying: there was no going back. Her life had never been as simple as she had imagined. It had always been tied to something bigger, something far more dangerous. And now, with Ethan caught in the middle, the weight of it all bore down on her like a storm.

And somewhere, deep inside, a small part of her still believed there was hope. But that hope was fragile, like a thread holding her to a reality she wasn't sure she could survive.

Eight

Obsession

The small, dimly lit room felt like a cage. A trap that Lily couldn't escape, no matter how hard she tried. It was sterile and cold, the walls lined with outdated monitors and blinking lights, the air heavy with the scent of metal and machinery. In the center of the room, a large glass tank stood—its contents obscured by a thick layer of fog. But Lily didn't need to see what was inside to understand the gravity of the situation. She could feel it in the air. The tension. The silent hum of machines working beneath the surface, pushing the boundaries of something dark and unknown.

She could hear her heartbeat pounding in her ears as she stood at the edge of the tank, her fingers trembling at her sides. Amelia had led her here—somewhere deep within the abandoned complex. Somewhere hidden from the eyes of the world. It was in these very shadows that everything she had tried to escape had finally caught up with her. It was here, in this place, that she would learn more about herself than she ever wanted to know.

"Do you understand now?" Amelia's voice cut through the silence, sharp and commanding.

Lily didn't answer right away. She couldn't. She couldn't form the words, couldn't make sense of what was unfolding in front of her. Amelia's words were sharp, but it wasn't the words themselves that held her captive. It was the truth behind them. The truth that was now staring her in the face.

Amelia stepped closer, her eyes fixed on the tank. "Everything that's happened—the people following you, the danger you're in—it's all because of what's inside there," she said, pointing to the fog-covered tank. "What you're about to see will change everything. Your life won't be the same again. But you need to understand what you're dealing with."

Lily's chest tightened, a knot of fear growing in her stomach. Her gaze flickered to the tank once again. She didn't want to look. Didn't want to see whatever was inside. But she had to. She had to know what was truly at stake. She had already come this far. There was no turning back now.

"Don't be afraid," Amelia said softly, though her voice was tinged with something else—something darker. "What's in there is a part of you. A part of your past. A part of your bloodline."

Lily's breath caught in her throat. A part of her bloodline? She felt the world around her tilt, spinning as she tried to piece together the fragments of this nightmare. Her family. Her legacy. But how could this be true? What did Amelia mean? What was in the tank?

Slowly, reluctantly, she reached forward, pulling aside the edge of the thick, foggy veil that obscured the tank. The air inside was cool, and a chill ran down her spine as the contents became visible. She gasped, her hand flying to her mouth to stifle the noise that threatened to escape.

Inside the tank was a woman. At least, that's what it looked like—though not quite human. The figure was suspended in the thick, viscous liquid, her body pale and lifeless, her hair drifting around her like seaweed in water. She looked like a ghost—fragile, haunting, and so eerily familiar that Lily's blood ran cold.

"Who is she?" Lily whispered, her voice trembling as she fought to hold back the surge of panic rising in her chest. "What is this?"

Amelia stood beside her, her eyes not leaving the tank. "This is your legacy, Lily. This is why you were born. This woman is the reason you're being hunted. The reason your family's name is tied to something much darker than you ever realized."

Lily shook her head, the words not fully making sense to her. "No. This… this isn't possible." Her breath was coming in shallow gasps as she looked at the woman inside the tank. Her heart pounded louder in her chest, each beat like a drum signaling the inevitable. "How is this connected to me?"

Amelia's face was unreadable as she looked down at the floor for a moment, gathering her thoughts. "The woman you see in that tank is a result of an experiment—a long-forgotten project from your family's past. Your ancestors were not just wealthy. They were also involved in scientific experimentation, creating something beyond human comprehension. Something that, when activated, would change the course of history."

Lily's mind was reeling, her head spinning with the weight of Amelia's words. "My family... they did this?" she whispered in disbelief.

"Not your immediate family. But your bloodline. Your ancestors," Amelia corrected, her voice low. "Your family's wealth is only part of the picture. The Hartwell name is tied to something far more dangerous, far more powerful than you can imagine. And this woman"—Amelia nodded toward the tank—"was the first attempt. She was created from a combination of genetic manipulation and forbidden science. She was meant to be the prototype for something greater."

Lily stepped back, shaking her head. "You're telling me this is real? That my family was involved in... in genetic manipulation?"

"Yes," Amelia replied, her eyes hardening. "And it's not just about the past. This project wasn't abandoned. It was covered up. Erased. Your family wanted to bury it, to hide it from the world. But they couldn't destroy what they had created. It was too powerful. And now, you're being pulled into this because you carry their legacy."

Lily's head spun. Her breath came in shallow, frantic gasps as she tried to process the magnitude of what Amelia was saying. The weight of it all pressed in on her—her family, her bloodline, a legacy she had never known. She had thought she had escaped it. She had thought she had left behind the wealthy, suffocating life her parents had imposed on her. But now, she realized she couldn't escape what ran through her veins.

"You're saying I'm connected to this?" she asked, her voice a whisper. "To this experiment? To this woman?"

"Yes," Amelia said, her voice grave. "You are the key. The bloodline that carries the potential for this experiment to succeed. You're a direct descendant of those who created this. Your connection to her... to this experiment... it's why people are after you. They want to use you to finish what was started."

Lily stepped back, her mind reeling. She could hardly breathe, the weight of the truth crushing down on her. The woman in the tank—she could see it now. The resemblance. The slight tilt of her face, the curve of her cheekbones. She had always known there was something different about her. Something buried deep within her family's history, but she never could have imagined that it was something so terrifying.

"Why me?" Lily asked, her voice barely audible. "Why not someone else?"

Amelia turned toward her, her gaze intense. "Because you are the last. The last of your family's bloodline to carry the gene—the gene that ties you to this experiment. They've been watching you for years, waiting for the right moment to activate it. And now, it's time."

Lily felt the room closing in on her. She was trapped—trapped in a life she never wanted, tied to a legacy she could never escape. Everything she had fought for, everything she had hoped to leave behind, was now part of her, buried in her blood. She wasn't just running from her family. She was running from herself. From who she really was.

The door to the lab suddenly burst open, and Lily's heart skipped a beat. She spun around to see two men standing in the doorway, their faces hidden in the shadows. They moved with precision, their eyes fixed on Lily as they stepped into the room.

"Amelia," one of the men said, his voice cold and commanding. "Is she ready?"

Amelia's expression remained unchanged as she nodded. "She's the one. It's time to begin."

Lily felt her breath catch in her throat. What did that mean? Begin what? What were they going to do to her?

Before she could react, one of the men moved quickly toward her, gripping her arm in a vise-like hold. The other man followed, his hand hovering near a device on the table that hummed with a low, dangerous power.

"You can't do this!" Lily shouted, trying to break free. "You don't understand! I'm not part of this!"

Amelia stepped forward, her face unreadable. "You're already part of it, Lily. Whether you like it or not."

And just like that, Lily realized the truth. There was no escape. Not from her family. Not from the experiments. Not from the dark, tangled world she had tried so hard to leave behind. The only choice left was to survive it.

And that, she knew, was going to be the hardest thing she'd ever done.

Nine

Another Life

Lily's mind raced as the men moved toward her, their cold hands gripping her arms with iron strength. The room felt smaller with each passing second, the walls pressing in around her as she struggled to breathe. She could feel the pulse of something dark rising within her, a storm she couldn't control, and it filled her with terror. This wasn't just about her anymore. This was about something far more dangerous, something that ran through her veins—something that had been hidden for generations. She was at the center of it now, and there was no escape.

"Let go of me!" Lily screamed, her voice cracking with desperation, but the men barely flinched. Their hands didn't loosen, didn't give an inch. They weren't there to negotiate. They weren't there to listen.

One of the men spoke in a low voice, his breath cold against her ear. "You're not in control anymore, Lily. It's time for you to understand that."

Lily's heart pounded, each beat echoing in her chest. She had thought she could escape. She had thought that by leaving her old life behind, by shedding the skin of Isabella Hartwell, she could outrun the legacy that her family had burdened her with. But she had been wrong. She couldn't outrun the truth. She couldn't outrun the past.

Amelia stepped forward, her eyes cold and calculating. She looked at Lily like someone watching an experiment unfold, a silent observer in a room full of chaos. "It's for the greater good," she said softly, her voice devoid of emotion. "You'll understand soon enough. Everything you're feeling right now is part of the process. It has to be this way."

Lily's mind was reeling, trying to make sense of everything she was hearing. The words were fragments, pieces of a puzzle that refused to fit together. She wanted to scream, to run, to make sense of what was happening to her, but the fear, the anxiety, the sheer weight of it all seemed to swallow her whole.

"What do you want from me?" Lily gasped, her voice hoarse, her eyes wild with fear. "What are you going to do to me?"

Amelia stepped closer, her presence almost suffocating in the confined space of the lab. She placed a hand gently on the glass tank, her fingers tracing the surface as she spoke. "You've always had the answers, Lily. You've just never been ready to face them. Your family created this, not just for wealth, not just for power. They created this to bring you to this point, to this moment."

Lily's eyes darted to the tank, her mind struggling to understand the horrific connection between herself and the woman inside. She could see the faint outline of the woman's face beneath the foggy liquid, her eyes closed, her body suspended in the eerie stillness. It was almost like a reflection of Lily's own life—a life frozen in time, a life waiting to be awakened, waiting to be controlled.

"No!" Lily cried out, shaking her head violently. "I'm not like her. I'm not some… some experiment!"

Amelia's expression didn't change. She looked at Lily with cold, unwavering eyes, as if she had heard these words countless times before. "You are. You always have been. And you will continue to be until you accept what you are."

Lily struggled against the men holding her, her body straining with every ounce of energy she had left. But their grip was unyielding, and she knew there was nothing she could do to break free. She was powerless. Helpless. She could feel it now, deep in her bones—the realization that no matter how far she ran, no matter how much she tried to bury her past, she could never escape the truth of who she was.

The room was silent for a moment, the only sound the soft hum of the machines around them. Then, one of the men spoke, his voice low and mechanical. "It's time. The procedure is ready."

Lily's heart stopped. "Procedure?" she echoed, barely able to speak. "What are you talking about? What do you mean, ready?"

The second man, the one with cold, calculating eyes, stepped forward, his hand resting on the machine that hummed steadily in the corner of the room. He didn't look at her as he spoke. "The activation is complete. We're starting the process now. You're the final piece of the puzzle."

Lily's breath hitched in her chest as her body tensed, her mind racing. "No... I can't do this. I won't."

But it was too late. She could already feel the familiar sense of helplessness creeping in, the realization that she was trapped, that her fate had been sealed long before she had ever stepped into this dark, forgotten place.

"Please," she whispered, her voice breaking. "I don't want this. I never asked for this. I didn't ask for any of it."

Amelia's cold gaze met hers, unyielding, unforgiving. "You don't get to choose, Lily. Not anymore."

The men moved quickly, pulling her toward the table in the center of the room. The machines around them buzzed to life, their eerie glow reflecting in Lily's wide, terrified eyes. Her heart raced, thundering in her chest as she tried to resist, to fight back, but it was useless. They were stronger. They were in control. And there was nothing she could do to stop it.

As they strapped her down to the cold metal table, the buzzing of the machines grew louder, filling the room with an oppressive hum that seemed to vibrate through her entire body. She could feel the cold metal against her skin, could feel the heat of the machines as they began their work.

Her mind was a blur of panic, her body fighting against the restraints, but there was no escape. She was trapped, caught in a web of secrets and lies, a web that her family had woven long before she had ever been born. And now, as the machines began their process, as the procedure began to unfold, she realized with a sickening certainty that she was not just a victim. She was the key.

The first shock of electricity sent a jolt through her body, her muscles locking as she gasped in pain. The world around her spun, a blur of lights and shadows. She could hear her own heartbeat, the rush of blood in her ears, as the machines worked their dark magic. Each pulse felt like it was tearing her apart, pulling at the very fabric of who she was.

"No!" she screamed, the sound ragged in her throat. "Please, stop! I'm not—"

But the machines didn't stop. They didn't care about her pleas. They didn't care about the woman she had tried to become, the life she had fought for. They were only interested in one thing: the power she carried within her, the power that had been passed down through her bloodline for generations.

Lily's body trembled as the pain intensified, each shock more excruciating than the last. She could feel something inside her shifting, a force she couldn't control, something dark and powerful beginning to stir. It was like her entire world was being turned upside down, like her very DNA was being rewritten, rewritten by the hands of those who had planned this for years.

"Stop!" Lily gasped, her voice breaking as the last remnants of her strength began to fade. "Please… stop…"

But Amelia's cold, impassive gaze was the last thing she saw before everything went black.

In that moment, the world around her disappeared—everything she had known, everything she had hoped for. The woman inside the tank. Her family. The life she had left behind. It all faded into darkness.

And Lily realized with a sickening clarity that she was no longer just a victim of her past. She was part of it. A part of the experiment. A part of the legacy she had tried to escape. And no matter how hard she fought, she would never be free of it.

Not now.

Not ever.

The procedure was complete.

And the transformation had begun.

Ten

The intimacy

Lily's eyes fluttered open to an oppressive silence, the kind that presses in from all sides, making every breath feel like a violation of the stillness. The sterile smell of the lab was still thick in the air, mingling with something darker—something metallic, a tang of blood that made her stomach churn. She could feel the coldness of the metal table beneath her, her body stiff and aching from the restraints that had held her. The pulse of the machines had stopped, but their presence lingered, suffocating her with their hum.

For a moment, she wasn't sure where she was. The world felt foreign, detached. Her head spun with a dizziness that made her vision blur, her thoughts fragmented like broken glass. What had happened? What had they done to her?

As she struggled to sit up, the ache in her body flared, sharp

The intimacy

and searing, and she winced. Her limbs felt heavy, as though they no longer belonged to her. She tried to lift her hands, but they trembled violently, uncooperative, as if the muscles had forgotten how to obey. She blinked rapidly, trying to clear her mind, trying to pull herself together, but the disorientation was overwhelming.

The door to the lab opened, its screeching hinges cutting through the silence. She froze, her breath catching in her throat. Someone was coming. She wasn't sure if she was ready to face whoever it was, but there was no time to prepare. The figure that entered was a shadow at first, a silhouette against the harsh, fluorescent lights of the hallway. But as the door clicked shut behind them, the figure stepped into the room, and Lily's heart skipped a beat.

It was Ethan.

His eyes locked with hers across the room, and for a moment, neither of them moved. The tension between them was thick, palpable. Ethan looked different—his face was more drawn, his expression troubled, but there was something else in his eyes. Something unfamiliar. A depth that made her wonder if he had known all along what she had been running from, what she had tried to keep hidden.

Lily opened her mouth to speak, but no words came out. Her throat was dry, raw from the screams she couldn't remember, from the pain that still lingered in her body. She swallowed hard, her hands instinctively pulling at the restraints that still held her to the table. It wasn't until she looked down that she realized they had been removed.

Ethan took a step forward, his gaze never leaving hers, and the weight of his presence seemed to fill the room, making it feel smaller, suffocating. "Lily," he said softly, his voice thick with an emotion she couldn't name. "What have they done to you?"

The words hit her like a punch, and for the first time since she had woken up, she felt the overwhelming need to explain, to make him understand. But how could she? How could she make him understand the truth of what had happened to her, to what was still happening?

"I don't…" Her voice faltered, weak and unsteady. "I don't know, Ethan. I don't know what they've done. I…" She trailed off, her mind reeling, trying to piece together the fragments of what had happened. The procedure. The shock. The transformation. But the pieces didn't fit together. The answers she sought felt just out of reach, like trying to hold onto a dream that slipped through her fingers every time she tried to grasp it.

Ethan stepped closer, his presence like a magnet pulling her toward him. His hand reached out, his fingers brushing her face in a touch so soft, so gentle, it made her heart ache. She wanted to pull away, to keep the distance between them, to protect him from whatever darkness had invaded her life. But she couldn't. She couldn't pull away from him, not now. Not when everything she had felt before, everything she had wanted, was slipping through her hands like sand.

"I'm so sorry," Ethan whispered, his voice breaking. "I had

no idea. I had no idea what you were really running from. I thought…" He trailed off, shaking his head as if the words couldn't form properly. "I thought you just wanted to get away from your family. But this… This is so much more than that."

Lily closed her eyes, her breath shallow as she fought to control the emotions that were threatening to overwhelm her. How could she explain it? How could she tell him what was happening inside of her, what was waking up in her blood, in her mind? The truth felt too monstrous to voice. Too overwhelming to bear.

"I didn't want this," she said, her voice barely a whisper. "I never asked for this. I never asked for any of it."

Ethan's hand lingered on her cheek, his touch warm, a stark contrast to the coldness that still clung to her skin. His gaze softened, and for a brief moment, Lily saw the man she had met so many weeks ago. The man who had cared for her, who had shown her kindness when no one else had. The man who had made her feel seen.

"I know," he said gently. "I know you didn't."

His fingers drifted down to her hand, and before she could stop herself, before she could pull away, he wrapped his fingers around hers, his grip firm and reassuring. It was a simple touch, but it felt like everything—like a lifeline she hadn't known she needed. For a moment, she forgot about the tanks, the machines, the dark legacy that had trapped her in this place. She forgot about everything but the way his hand felt in hers.

Lily didn't realize how badly she had wanted this—how badly she had wanted him—until he was here, so close, so real. The emotions that had been locked away for so long surged to the surface, a tidal wave she couldn't stop. The fear, the longing, the desire. All of it mixed together, pulling her toward him in a way that terrified her. But she couldn't stop herself. She didn't want to.

Her breath hitched in her chest as Ethan leaned in, his face inches from hers, his lips so close that she could feel the warmth of his breath. For a heartbeat, time seemed to freeze, and the entire world fell away. There was only the space between them, filled with an electric tension that threatened to explode. She knew what was coming. She could feel it in the way her heart raced, in the way his thumb brushed over her skin, in the way his eyes darkened with something she couldn't name but desperately wanted.

And then, without thinking, she closed the distance between them. The kiss was soft at first—tentative, almost as if they were both unsure, hesitant, testing the waters. But soon, it deepened, and everything changed. It was like the floodgates had opened. The kiss was desperate, urgent, a release of everything they had been holding back. The emotions. The pain. The need. All of it poured into that one moment.

Lily's hands gripped his shoulders, pulling him closer, needing the connection, needing to feel something—anything—to prove that she was still alive, still capable of love despite everything that had happened to her, despite the darkness that had invaded her life.

The intimacy

Ethan responded with equal intensity, his hands sliding to her back, pulling her into him as if he couldn't get close enough. Their kiss was a chaotic mix of urgency and tenderness, an unspoken promise that despite the horrors surrounding them, despite the broken world they found themselves in, there was something pure between them. Something real.

But then, just as quickly as it had started, it ended. Lily pulled away, her chest heaving as she tried to regain control of herself, her emotions still raw and unhinged. She couldn't think clearly. Couldn't process what had just happened. She had crossed a line, a line that she didn't know how to come back from.

Ethan's breath was ragged, his eyes wild with something that mirrored her own confusion. "Lily…" he whispered, his voice hoarse. "I don't—"

"I'm sorry," she cut him off, stepping back, her face flushed, her hands trembling. "I can't. I… I don't know what this is, Ethan. I don't know who I am anymore."

He looked at her, his expression unreadable, but there was a flicker of something in his eyes. Something that told her he understood.

"You don't have to know right now," he said quietly. "I'm not going anywhere. Whatever happens next, we'll face it together."

Lily looked at him, her heart pounding in her chest. She wanted to believe him. She wanted to believe that there was still hope for them. But the truth was, she didn't know if there could be. Not with everything that was coming for her. Not with everything she had already lost.

And yet, in that moment, with Ethan standing in front of her, his hand reaching for hers once again, she felt something she hadn't felt in so long. For the first time in a long time, she felt like maybe—just maybe—she wasn't as alone as she thought.

Eleven

Fight

Lily stood at the edge of the rooftop, staring out at the sprawling city below. The wind tugged at her hair, the cool night air biting at her skin, but she barely felt it. Her thoughts were elsewhere—twisted, fractured, swirling around the dark and painful truth she had come to understand in the past few days. She felt like a stranger in her own body, her past and present colliding in ways she couldn't control. And the truth of it all—the legacy she was tied to, the genetic anomaly she carried inside of her—had only become clearer since the procedure.

The kiss with Ethan had felt like a lifeline, a spark of humanity in a world that had suddenly turned alien, but now, as she stood there, looking at the world she knew and felt so far from, she realized the true weight of the decision she had made. There was no going back. No simple undoing of the past. The transformation wasn't just in her body—it was in her soul. She could feel it, like a dark presence inside of her, pushing against her, waiting to break free.

The procedure had been more than just a series of shocks, more than just an experiment in genetic manipulation. It had been a key—a key to something that had been locked away for centuries. The project her ancestors had started wasn't just about power, it was about something deeper, something that had the potential to unravel the very fabric of reality itself. She didn't understand it yet, but she knew she was at the center of it. And the consequences of that knowledge were too heavy to bear.

Her eyes scanned the horizon, the lights of the city flickering like stars in a vast, dark sky. It should have been comforting. It should have been familiar. But instead, the city felt like a cage, the buildings and streets mere walls closing in on her. She had been living a lie for so long, wearing the mask of Isabella Hartwell, the perfect heiress, the perfect daughter. But now, the mask was gone. The illusion shattered. And what remained was something far darker, something far more dangerous than she had ever imagined.

The soft click of a door opening behind her broke the silence. She didn't need to turn around to know who it was. She felt him before she saw him—Ethan. His presence was like a warmth in the cold night, pulling her back from the edge of her thoughts, grounding her when everything inside her seemed to be spiraling out of control.

Fight

"I thought I'd find you up here," Ethan said softly, his voice carrying the weight of a thousand unspoken words. He stepped beside her, his eyes scanning the city below, but she could feel his attention on her. The way he always looked at her, as if trying to see into the parts of her she didn't want to reveal.

Lily didn't respond right away. She just stared out at the city, her heart heavy. There were too many questions swirling in her mind, too many things she didn't understand. But there was one thing that stood out above all else: Ethan. He had seen her. Really seen her. Not just the mask, not just the legacy. He had seen the real her, the part of her that she had hidden away for so long. The part of her that was still human.

"You're not the same, are you?" Ethan asked, his voice gentle but firm. "I can feel it. Something's different. Something's changed inside of you."

Lily turned to face him, her eyes meeting his. For the first time in what felt like forever, she didn't feel like she was pretending. She wasn't wearing a mask, she wasn't playing a role. She was just... Lily. And Ethan was there, seeing her for who she really was. The weight of his gaze made her stomach tighten, and for a brief moment, she almost wished she could go back. Back to the way things had been before she had learned the truth. Before she had learned what she really was.

"I don't know what's happening to me," she said, her voice breaking. "I don't know who I am anymore. I don't know if I ever really did."

Ethan took a step closer, his hand reaching out to gently touch her arm. His fingers were warm, steady. Reassuring. "You're still you, Lily. Whatever's happened, whatever they've done to you, it doesn't change who you are. You're the woman I know. The woman I—" He stopped himself, his face flushing slightly. "The woman I care about."

The words hung in the air between them, thick with the unspoken truth of what had been growing between them, what had been left unsaid. For a moment, Lily forgot about the storm inside her, forgot about the genetic manipulation, the experiment, the forces that had been set into motion long before she was born. All she could focus on was Ethan. The way his touch made her feel safe, even when everything around them was crumbling.

But the truth was still there, hovering in the background, threatening to tear them apart. She couldn't ignore it. She couldn't ignore what she had learned, what she had become.

"Ethan," she whispered, her voice trembling. "I'm not who you think I am. I'm not just the woman you've been falling for. I'm… I'm part of something much darker. Something dangerous."

He frowned, his brow furrowing as he took a step back. "What do you mean?"

Lily closed her eyes, the weight of her confession pressing on her chest. "I'm part of a project. A project my family started a long time ago. It's not just about power. It's about time. About bending reality itself. The procedure they did on me—

it activated something inside me, something that was meant to stay dormant. It's a part of me, and it's... it's changing everything."

Ethan was silent for a moment, his gaze searching her face as if trying to make sense of what she had just said. He reached out again, his hand finding hers. "Lily, I don't care what's in your bloodline, or what they've done to you. You're still you. I know who you are. And I—" He stopped, his voice faltering as he looked into her eyes. "I'm not going anywhere."

But Lily couldn't meet his gaze. She felt the weight of his words, the comfort of his presence, and yet, deep inside her, there was a gnawing fear that wouldn't go away. She wasn't the same. Not anymore. And no matter how hard she tried to deny it, no matter how much she wanted to hold on to the life she had known, the truth was inescapable.

The sound of footsteps approaching from behind them interrupted the moment. Both Lily and Ethan turned to see Amelia standing at the entrance to the rooftop, her expression unreadable. She had been silent for so long, her presence like a shadow that always seemed to loom just out of reach. And now, here she was, stepping into the light, her eyes cold and calculating as always.

"I see you've shared your little secret with him," Amelia said, her voice sharp and clipped. "I didn't think it would take this long for you to realize what's happening. But it's clear now. You've activated something inside of you, Lily. Something that's much bigger than both of you."

The Disguised Heart of a Heiress

Lily's heart sank. "What do you mean?" she asked, her voice barely a whisper. The last thing she needed was more uncertainty. She didn't know how much longer she could bear the weight of it all.

Amelia stepped forward, her heels clicking on the pavement as she closed the distance between them. "What you're feeling, what you're experiencing—it's the beginning. The rift is forming. The reality you know, the life you think you're living, it's slipping away. The procedure didn't just activate your genetic makeup. It began the process of shifting the boundaries of time itself. You're tied to something far more powerful than you could ever imagine, and as it grows inside you, so does the danger."

Lily shook her head, the words impossible to grasp, like a thread unraveling from the fabric of her life. "No. This can't be happening. I can't be part of this. I can't be part of something that's going to destroy everything."

Amelia's eyes softened for a moment, but the hardness in her voice remained. "You don't have a choice. This isn't about you anymore. It never was. You are the catalyst, Lily. And once the rift is fully formed, once the timeline begins to fracture… there will be no going back."

Lily took a step back, her mind whirling with the weight of it all. The world she knew, the life she had fought so hard to escape, was slipping through her fingers. And now, the rift in the fabric of time—this dark force that she had unknowingly activated—was threatening to tear everything apart.

Fight

As the wind whipped around them, Lily felt a strange calm settle over her. She wasn't alone. Not yet. And as long as Ethan was by her side, maybe—just maybe—they could find a way to stop it. To stop whatever was coming. But the truth was, she didn't know if she had the power to control it. And as the rift began to spread, as the fabric of reality began to tear, she realized that the life she had known—everything she had taken for granted—was already slipping away.

Twelve

The Watchers

The night had swallowed the city whole, casting a deep shadow over the streets below. Lily stood in the sterile confines of the abandoned lab, the weight of Amelia's words pressing down on her chest like an anvil. She couldn't breathe. She couldn't think. All she could do was listen, listen to the ticking of the clock on the wall, and the steady hum of the machines that had once been part of a life she was trying to escape.

"Are you ready to face it?" Amelia's voice sliced through the silence, her words sharp like a blade.

Lily didn't answer right away. How could she? How could anyone truly be ready for what awaited her? A rift in the fabric of time itself. She was at the center of it, tangled in a web of scientific experiments, bloodlines, and forces beyond her comprehension. But there was more to it than that. There was something else, something lurking just beneath the surface of her thoughts, waiting for her to acknowledge it. It was fear, yes. But it was also something darker. A power she could feel stirring inside of her, a presence that pulsed beneath her skin like an echo of something ancient, something that had been buried in the depths of her DNA for centuries.

Amelia moved toward the console, her fingers dancing over the buttons with practiced ease. "Time is running out," she said quietly, her voice laden with urgency. "We don't have the luxury of waiting for you to figure this out. We need you to step into this. Now."

Lily's gaze flickered to the small glass tank in the corner of the room—the place where she had first seen the woman who was supposed to be her ancestor. The woman who had been subjected to the same experiments. The woman who, in some twisted way, was part of her bloodline. Part of the power that now coursed through her.

"Do you ever wonder if it's worth it?" Lily asked, her voice barely above a whisper. "If any of this… any of this is worth it? I didn't ask for this. I didn't choose to be a part of this experiment. I didn't choose to be tied to this legacy."

Amelia paused, her fingers stilling on the console for a moment. "Sometimes," she said slowly, "the things we inherit are beyond our control. But we can choose how we respond to them. You have power, Lily. A power that goes beyond anything you can imagine. And you're not alone in this."

Lily clenched her fists, feeling the sudden surge of that power inside her again. It was an overwhelming sensation, like a current running through her veins, both electrifying and suffocating at the same time. She could feel it fighting for control, for dominance, and she wasn't sure if she was strong enough to hold it back. She had never asked for this. She had never wanted to be the one to carry the weight of this legacy.

But now, standing in the midst of it all, with Ethan's words echoing in her mind—I'm not going anywhere—she realized that maybe there was something more she could fight for. Maybe there was a way to control it, to stop it, to rewrite the narrative of her life before it was too late.

"I don't even know who I am anymore," Lily murmured, her voice cracking under the weight of it all.

"You're still you," Amelia replied, her voice steady, unwavering. "You're still Lily Williams. But now, you have the chance to choose who you will become. And you're not alone."

Lily glanced at Amelia, her brow furrowing. "You keep saying that, but I don't believe you. Not yet. How can I trust you?"

Amelia's eyes softened, and for the first time, Lily saw a flicker of something other than calculation in her eyes—something that resembled empathy. "You don't have to trust me. You just have to trust yourself."

The words hung in the air, thick with meaning. Trust herself. She wanted to, so badly. But how could she? Everything she had believed, everything she had known about herself, had been shattered. She wasn't just running from her family anymore—she was running from a future that she couldn't control. A future that was now tied to a rift in time itself.

"I don't even know what to do with this power," Lily confessed, her voice barely audible. "It feels like it's consuming me."

"That's because you're fighting it," Amelia said, her voice calm, almost motherly. "You've spent your whole life fighting the truth. Fighting the blood that runs through your veins. You can't fight it anymore. You have to embrace it."

Lily took a step back, shaking her head. "No. I can't. This is too much. I can't handle it."

Amelia was silent for a moment, and when she spoke again, her voice was softer. "You don't have a choice anymore, Lily. The watchers are already closing in. They know what you are, and they'll stop at nothing to control you. To control this. But you can control it. You can choose to stop it."

The tension in the room seemed to crackle, the air growing heavier with each word Amelia spoke. Lily's chest tightened as the weight of her words sank in. The watchers. They had been watching her, monitoring her every move since the procedure. They were the ones pulling the strings behind the scenes. The ones who had engineered the rift in the first place. And they weren't just after her—they were after everything she represented.

Suddenly, a sharp noise pierced the silence, the sound of metal scraping against metal. Lily turned toward the door, her heart racing. There was no mistaking it now. The watchers had arrived. They were here.

Amelia stepped in front of her, her body a shield as the door to the lab flew open. The men who stepped inside were tall, dressed in dark suits that seemed to absorb the light around them. Their faces were obscured by shadows, their eyes cold and unfeeling. They moved with the precision of hunters, their eyes scanning the room for their prey.

Lily's breath caught in her throat. This was it. This was the moment when everything she had tried to escape came crashing down on her. She could feel the power within her surging again, the darkness threatening to consume her, to take control. But she couldn't let it. She couldn't let them see her like this.

"What do you want?" Lily demanded, her voice shaking with both fear and defiance.

The man at the front of the group stepped forward, his expression unreadable. "We're here for what's ours," he said, his voice low and steady. "The rift is destabilizing, and we need you to fix it. Now."

Lily's heart pounded in her chest as she took a step back, glancing at Amelia. "Fix it? How? What do you mean?"

The man didn't answer right away. Instead, he stepped closer, his eyes locked onto Lily's. "You are the key, Lily. You always have been. We've been watching you for years, waiting for the right moment to strike. The moment when the rift would open fully. And now, we need you to finish it. We need you to stabilize it, or everything will unravel. You're the one who can make this right."

Lily shook her head, a cold sweat breaking out on her forehead. "I don't know how to do that. I don't even know what I am!"

The man's gaze hardened, his voice cutting through the air like a blade. "You're the daughter of a legacy that's been hidden from the world. The rift, the power—it's all inside of you. And you will fix it, or we will make you."

Lily took a step back, her mind reeling, her breath coming in short, panicked gasps. She had never felt more powerless in her life. They had known. They had been watching her all along. And now, they were demanding the one thing she didn't have—the ability to control the rift.

"Please," she whispered, her voice trembling. "I don't know what you want from me. I don't know how to fix this."

The man's lips twisted into a cold smile, and for the first time, Lily saw a flicker of something in his eyes—something that wasn't just cold indifference. There was something darker, something far more dangerous.

"You don't need to know how, Lily," he said softly. "You just need to do it."

The room seemed to tilt as the world around Lily collapsed into chaos. The rift. The watchers. The power inside her. All of it was closing in on her, forcing her to make a choice. A choice she wasn't ready to make.

And yet, deep down, she knew there was only one way forward. Only one path that could lead her to the truth. Only one path that could stop the rift from tearing everything apart.

But at what cost? And who would be left standing when it was all over?

Thirteen

Falling

The air in the lab was thick with tension, like the calm before a storm. Lily could feel it wrapping around her, squeezing the breath from her chest. The men—the watchers—moved with a purpose, their eyes cold and calculating, their presence a silent command that she couldn't ignore. She had no choice now. No choice but to play along, to pretend she understood even a fraction of what was happening. They weren't here to negotiate. They weren't here to talk.

She was the key.

The thought echoed in her mind like a mantra. She was the one they needed. She was the one who could either stabilize the rift or allow it to tear everything apart.

Her gaze flicked to Amelia, standing to her left, her arms crossed over her chest, eyes narrowing with suspicion as she watched the watchers. Amelia's calm demeanor contrasted sharply with the tension building in the room. She knew more than she was letting on. Lily had no doubt about that. But what exactly was she hiding? What did she know about the rift, and how to stop it?

"Lily," the lead watcher said, his voice low and commanding. "You know what has to happen. We've waited too long for this."

Lily's hands trembled at her sides. The words felt foreign on her tongue. "I don't know how to fix it," she whispered, her voice breaking. "I don't even know what I am anymore."

The watcher's eyes glinted with something darker—impatience, perhaps, or something more sinister. "You are the product of centuries of research. You are the culmination of everything your bloodline has been working toward. You will fix this."

The words felt like a blade to her chest. A deep, cutting blow. How could she fix something she didn't even understand? How could she control the rift when it had always felt like something beyond her reach?

Amelia stepped forward, her voice steady but sharp. "She doesn't owe you anything."

The watcher's expression hardened, his gaze flicking to Amelia with contempt. "She owes us everything. You all do." He turned back to Lily, his voice dropping to a whisper. "You are not the first to bear this power, Lily. There have been others before you.

Falling

They failed. They couldn't control it. They couldn't manage the rift."

Lily's stomach turned as the weight of his words sank in. Others? How many others had been sacrificed for this? How many had been manipulated, experimented on, only to fail? And now, it was her turn. It was her responsibility to fix a problem she didn't even understand.

"I can't do this," she whispered, her voice barely audible.

"You can," the watcher insisted, stepping closer, his shadow falling over her. "You must. If you don't—if you refuse—everything will collapse. The rift will consume everything you know. Everything you care about."

Lily's mind spun as the fear threatened to take over. She could feel the power inside her, pulsing with a rhythm of its own, a force that seemed to be growing stronger, more insistent with every passing second. The rift, the connection to the past, the experiments—everything she had learned about herself in the past weeks, everything that had shaped her reality, was rushing at her now, like a tidal wave.

She closed her eyes, trying to steady her breath, trying to fight back the panic. *I don't want this. I don't want this to be my fate.*

The moment she thought it, the room seemed to shift. The world around her warped and flickered like a glitch in the fabric of reality itself. The watchers were still there, but they were suddenly… distant. Their faces twisted, flickering like broken images. The walls of the lab blurred, the edges of the room pulling away like smoke.

Lily opened her eyes, but the world she knew was gone. She was no longer standing in the sterile lab. Instead, she was surrounded by a vast, endless void—blackness stretching out in all directions, broken only by flashes of light that seemed to pulse like distant stars. The sound of her breathing was loud in the silence, echoing through the void.

"What is this?" she whispered, her voice trembling. "Where am I?"

"Where you've always been," a voice answered.

She spun around, her heart racing as she saw the figure standing in the darkness. It was a woman. She was tall, slender, her features sharp and pale, like something out of a forgotten dream. Her eyes glowed with an unnatural light, and when she spoke again, her voice was both familiar and foreign.

"You've been running from this for so long," the woman said, her gaze piercing through Lily. "But you can't run anymore. It's time to face the truth."

Lily's pulse quickened. "Who are you?"

The woman didn't answer at first. She simply stared at Lily, her expression unreadable. Then, after a long, agonizing silence, she spoke again. "I am the first. The first of your bloodline to be part of the experiment. The first to be part of what you are."

Falling

Lily took a step back, her mind racing. "You... you're me?"

The woman shook her head, a cold smile curling on her lips. "No. I was what you were meant to be. But you're different. You're more than I ever could have been. And you're running out of time to understand it."

Lily's chest tightened, the fear threatening to choke her. "What do you want from me? What am I supposed to do?"

The woman's smile faded, her eyes hardening. "The rift is already here, Lily. It's already within you. But unless you can control it, unless you can unlock what lies beneath, it will consume you—and everything else."

Lily's breath caught in her throat. "How?"

The woman stepped forward, her eyes locked on Lily's with a strange intensity. "You must embrace it. The power. The blood. You are tied to it. You always have been. The rift is not just a rift in time—it's a rift in everything. It is the fabric of all things, and you are the key to its restoration—or its destruction."

Lily took another step back, her heart pounding. "I don't understand. How do I fix it? How do I control this... this power?"

The woman's expression softened, a faint flicker of something resembling pity crossing her face. "You don't. Not yet. You're not ready. But you will be. The rift needs you to make a choice."

The Disguised Heart of a Heiress

Lily's mind spun. A choice. What choice? There were no choices left. There was no escape.

"You will either learn to control the rift, to bind time to your will, or you will let it fracture, let it tear everything apart. Every reality, every moment will collapse into chaos. The rift will pull everything in. All of us."

Lily's legs weakened, and she stumbled back, her vision starting to blur. This was too much. This wasn't her. She wasn't meant to be this person—this weapon, this key to an ancient experiment. She wasn't ready to carry the weight of it all.

"I'm not ready," she whispered, the words slipping out of her mouth before she could stop them.

The woman stepped closer, her eyes boring into Lily's. "You don't have a choice. You're already part of this. You've always been part of it."

The world seemed to close in on Lily, the darkness pressing around her like a vice. The rift was inside of her, a force that she couldn't control, a force that was both terrifying and seductive. And now, in this strange place between realities, between time, she realized that the world she had known—the life she had been fighting to reclaim—was slipping away. Everything she had tried to protect, everything she had fought for, was caught in the crossfire of something far beyond her control.

"I can't," she whispered again, her voice breaking. "I can't do this."

Falling

The woman's expression softened, her gaze almost sympathetic. "You don't have a choice."

With that, the woman stepped forward, her cold hand reaching for Lily's. As the woman's fingers brushed her skin, everything went white.

A burst of light, like a thousand stars collapsing into one, erupted in front of her. And Lily was falling, falling through reality, through time itself.

She screamed, but the sound was swallowed by the vast emptiness around her, and she was lost to the void, pulled deeper into the heart of the rift. And as she fell, she understood the truth. She was the rift, the key. And she was about to make the choice that would determine everything.

She just didn't know if she could survive it.

Fourteen

Moments

The world was a blur. Everything around Lily fractured into a kaleidoscope of colors, light, and shadows as she fell through the void. The sensation was unlike anything she had ever felt—like being torn apart at the seams and then reassembled in a place that had no boundaries, no rules. The air was thick, impossibly heavy, and every breath she took seemed to suffocate her. The fear clawed at her, every instinct telling her to fight, to wake up, to escape. But there was nowhere to run. Nowhere to hide. She was trapped in the rift. And the rift was inside of her.

She didn't know how long she fell. Time had lost its meaning here. It felt like seconds, or perhaps hours. Her body ached, her mind screamed for clarity, but the only thing that remained was the overwhelming sense of being swallowed by something bigger than herself. The world she knew was slipping away. The rift was pulling her deeper into its dark heart, and she couldn't escape. She could feel the pull, the relentless tug of reality bending, warping around her as if time itself was unraveling.

And then, in an instant, everything stopped.

Lily gasped as her body was slammed back into a solid reality, the world suddenly stabilizing around her. She landed hard, her knees buckling as she hit the ground. For a moment, she could only sit there, gasping for air, her hands gripping the cold ground beneath her as she tried to process what had just happened. Her head was spinning, her heart still racing from the descent into the rift. She looked around, trying to make sense of her surroundings.

She was no longer in the void.

She was no longer in the lab.

She was... somewhere else.

The air around her was thick with the scent of earth and grass, and the familiar sound of wind rustling through trees filled her ears. She was in a forest. A dense, dark forest, the kind that felt both familiar and foreign at the same time. The trees loomed tall and thick, their branches stretching up into the sky, blocking out most of the light. It was quiet, save for the distant rustle of leaves and the soft hum of the world around her. But there was something about the place—something that felt wrong. The air tasted like memories, like something long lost and now forgotten.

A sudden noise made Lily freeze. Her breath caught in her throat, her heart pounding in her chest as she turned toward the sound. Someone was there. Someone was coming.

The trees parted, and there he was.

Ethan.

He stepped into the clearing, his figure emerging from the shadows like a ghost, his face expressionless. His eyes met hers, and for a moment, everything else seemed to fade into the background. The weight of the moment pressed down on her like a physical force, and her breath caught in her throat. She could feel the pull of him, the way he always had a way of grounding her, of making her feel like she wasn't completely alone. But this time... something was different.

His eyes locked with hers, a flicker of recognition passing between them. But there was something else, something deeper, in the way he looked at her. His brow furrowed, confusion clouding his face, as if he was seeing her for the first time.

"You... you're here," Ethan said, his voice shaky, unsure, as if he had expected her to be someone else. The words felt strange coming from him, like a puzzle piece that didn't quite fit. He took a step forward, his movements tentative. "How did you—where did you—?"

Lily shook her head, her hands trembling as she rose to her feet. "I don't know," she said, her voice barely above a whisper. "I don't know what's happening. I... I've been falling. Through time. Through reality."

Ethan's gaze never wavered, his eyes studying her as though he could somehow piece together the fragments of her scattered words. But his confusion deepened, and he took another step closer. "Lily… What is this? Where are we?"

Lily swallowed hard, her throat dry, her mind racing. She didn't know where they were. She didn't know how they had ended up here. All she knew was that everything had changed. The rift, the power, the legacy she couldn't escape—it was all crashing down around her, and she had no idea what it meant.

"I don't know," she said, her voice cracking with the weight of everything she had yet to understand. "But I think we've met before."

Ethan blinked, a confused frown pulling at the corners of his lips. "What are you talking about? Of course we've met before. You… you're the woman I've been looking for. The woman who—" He cut himself off, his eyes widening as if realizing something. His breath quickened, and he stepped back, as if suddenly unsure of who she was. "But you're different. You're not the same."

Lily's heart skipped a beat. She wanted to reach for him, to comfort him, to explain, but the words wouldn't come. Everything about this moment felt wrong. This wasn't the Ethan she had kissed, the Ethan who had been there for her when everything else seemed lost. This wasn't the man who had promised her they would face whatever was coming together.

This was someone else. Someone who didn't recognize her. Someone who wasn't meant to be here.

"I don't know what's happening, Ethan," Lily said, her voice trembling. "I don't know how we ended up here. I don't know what the rift is, or why it's affecting us. But I can feel it. I can feel it inside me, like a storm waiting to break. And I don't think I can stop it."

Ethan's eyes softened for a moment, a flicker of understanding passing between them. But then, just as quickly, that softness was gone. His expression hardened, his shoulders tensing. "The rift? What do you mean? What's going to happen?"

Lily closed her eyes, her head spinning with the weight of the truth she had yet to admit. "I don't know," she whispered again. "But I think it's already started. The rift is pulling everything apart, and I can feel it inside of me, Ethan. The past. The future. All of it is merging. It's happening now."

The forest around them seemed to pulse with a strange energy, a hum that vibrated through the ground beneath their feet. The air grew heavier, thick with a tension that Lily couldn't explain. She looked around, her eyes scanning the trees, the darkened woods closing in on them. There was something wrong with this place. Something that felt too familiar, too out of place.

"Lily," Ethan said, his voice low, his hands shaking as he reached out to her. "We need to figure this out. We need to stop the rift before it tears everything apart. Before it…"

He trailed off, his gaze flickering to the horizon. Lily followed his line of sight, her breath catching in her throat as the trees began to shift, the ground beneath them trembling. The sky above them was no longer a dark, starless void. It was bleeding, as if the fabric of the world itself was cracking, splitting open.

"No," she whispered, the words slipping from her lips in horror. "It's happening. The rift is pulling us in. It's pulling everything in."

The trees around them twisted and warped, their branches reaching toward them like skeletal hands, their shadows growing long and distorted. The air crackled with an electric charge, and Lily felt herself being drawn toward the darkness, the pull of the rift growing stronger, suffocating her.

"Ethan!" she screamed, reaching for him. "We need to get out of here. We need to—"

But it was too late. The world around them shattered.

The ground beneath their feet gave way, and in an instant, Lily and Ethan were falling—falling through time and space, through worlds that didn't exist, through realities that had never been meant to touch. The trees, the sky, the forest—all of it was gone, swallowed up by the rift. The dark, twisted force that had once been a whisper in Lily's mind was now a roar, a deafening crash of sound and light that threatened to tear everything apart.

And as they fell, Lily's last thought was this: She was no longer sure if she was falling through reality—or if reality itself was falling through her.

Fifteen

Found Love

~~~~~~

The fall was endless, a void that stretched into infinity, the swirling maelstrom of time, space, and reality blending into an impossible, chaotic storm. Lily couldn't breathe. She couldn't think. Everything that had ever made sense in her world—the people she loved, the life she had known—was falling away, slipping through her fingers like dust. Her body jerked violently, as if caught in a powerful undertow, but she had no control. She was being swept along by forces far beyond her understanding.

The weight of the rift pressed in on her, its dark power suffocating her, pulling at her very essence. She felt the rift in her bones, in her blood, and it was too much—too powerful. Her heartbeat thundered in her ears, matching the chaotic pulse of the world around her, and she thought, for a moment, that she might be losing herself. Losing everything. The pieces of her life were scattered, splintered, too fractured to repair. There was no sense to be made of it, no way to hold on.

And then, she felt him.

Ethan's hand found hers in the darkness, his grip firm, desperate. She didn't know how it was possible—how he was even there—but his presence, the warmth of his hand in hers, steadied her. It was the only thing that felt real anymore, the only thing that made sense.

"Lily!" His voice rang out in the chaos, a beacon in the dark, and she squeezed his hand harder, trying to steady herself. "We're still here. We're still together."

She didn't know how he could sound so calm, so sure, when everything around them was unraveling. The rift—her rift—was splitting open time itself, and she could feel the weight of it crushing her chest, threatening to rip her apart. Her heart pounded in her throat, each beat syncing with the disorienting, violent pull of the rift. But Ethan's voice—the sound of it—was like a lifeline.

"I don't know how much longer I can hold on," she said, her voice tight with fear. Her body felt weightless, her mind spinning, but his touch anchored her in the storm. She turned her head to look at him, even though the darkness made it hard to see anything clearly. "What is this? What's happening to us?"

"I don't know," Ethan said, his voice strained, but steady. He tightened his grip on her hand, his thumb brushing against hers, and Lily felt a spark of warmth in the cold, suffocating chaos. "But whatever it is, we're facing it together. You're not alone."

The words were like a balm to her panicked mind. She wanted to believe him, needed to believe him, but the rift was a force beyond anything they had ever faced. Time was no longer linear. Space was no longer fixed. The world, the very fabric of their reality, was bending and twisting around them, warping and tearing at the seams. She couldn't comprehend it. It was too much.

Suddenly, they were not falling anymore. The sensation stopped abruptly, as if they had collided with some unseen force. Lily gasped, her lungs filled with air she hadn't realized she had been starving for. Her body hit solid ground—no, not ground. A floor. She was lying flat on something hard, and for a moment, she was completely disoriented.

She blinked, trying to clear her vision. The chaotic, swirling void had disappeared, replaced by an eerie stillness. The air around them was no longer cold and suffocating. It was… still. Silent. Almost… perfect.

Lily slowly sat up, her head spinning, and gasped at the sight before her.

They were no longer in the rift. They weren't falling. They were standing in a vast, open space—a room, but not a room she recognized. The walls were made of smooth stone, glowing faintly with an ethereal light. The ceiling was impossibly high, stretching up into the darkness. There were no windows, no doors, no exit, only the strange, steady hum of energy vibrating in the air.

"What is this place?" she whispered, her voice a mixture of awe and fear.

"I don't know," Ethan replied, standing beside her, his eyes wide with disbelief. "But this… this doesn't feel like the rift anymore. It's different."

Lily nodded, her heart still racing in her chest. The sense of wrongness was palpable, the air thick with some unseen force that buzzed with energy. It felt both ancient and new, like a place untouched by time. She could feel it in the very air around her, a power that hummed just beneath the surface. It was strange. Otherworldly. And in the center of it all stood a single figure.

The figure stood alone in the center of the room, cloaked in shadow, their face hidden beneath a hood. They didn't move. Didn't speak. But their presence was undeniable, pressing in on them like a weight.

"Who are you?" Ethan asked, his voice firm but laced with uncertainty. His hand instinctively reached for Lily's, his fingers threading through hers.

The figure didn't respond at first. But after a long, heavy silence, they raised their hand slowly, revealing long, pale fingers that glowed faintly in the dim light. "You have come far, Lily Hartwell. Farther than most would ever dare."

Lily froze, her heart skipping a beat. The voice—it wasn't familiar, but it sent a shiver down her spine. How did this person know her name? How could they know who she was? She had no idea where she was, no idea how she had gotten here. But it was clear that whoever this figure was, they knew far more than they were letting on.

"Who are you?" Lily demanded, her voice shaky but filled with defiance. "What is this place? Why have we been brought here?"

The figure stepped forward, their movement fluid and graceful, like a shadow moving through the space. Their face remained hidden beneath the hood, but their presence was overwhelming. "This place is the nexus," they said, their voice like a whisper carried by the wind. "It is where time converges. Where the rift begins. And where the path to your true purpose lies."

Lily's breath caught in her throat. "The rift?" she repeated, her voice hoarse. "You mean the rift that's tearing apart everything?"

The figure's hand rose again, and a strange energy began to swirl around them, crackling in the air like static. "The rift was never meant to tear apart reality. It was meant to be a bridge. A path. A connection between the past and the future."

Lily shook her head, trying to make sense of the words. "A bridge? A connection? What are you talking about?"

"You are the bridge, Lily," the figure said, their voice low, almost soothing. "You are the one who can either stabilize the rift or let it consume everything."

The weight of the words hit Lily like a punch to the gut. She felt herself stagger back, her knees trembling. The rift wasn't just some random phenomenon. It wasn't just a tear in the fabric of time—it was her. She was at the center of it. The key. The one who could either fix everything or destroy it.

"But I don't know how!" she cried, her voice desperate. "I don't know what to do. I don't know how to control it!"

The figure tilted their head, and though their face remained hidden, Lily felt their gaze on her—deep, piercing, knowing. "You've always known, Lily. The answer has always been within you. You have only to accept it. To understand what you are."

Lily clenched her fists, the desperation threatening to overwhelm her. She wanted to run. She wanted to escape this place, this reality, but there was nowhere to go. There was only the figure in front of her, their words pulling her deeper into a fate she didn't understand. She didn't want to be the one who had to decide the fate of the world. She didn't want to carry the burden of the rift.

But as she stood there, staring at the figure in the center of the room, a part of her—a part of her she didn't know she had—knew the truth. She couldn't run anymore.

Ethan's grip on her hand tightened. She turned to him, her heart aching at the sight of him. His eyes were filled with the same fear, the same uncertainty, but there was something else there too. Something that told her he would stand by her. No matter what.

"This is it, isn't it?" she asked, her voice shaking with the weight of her own realization. "This is what I have to do. I have to face it."

Ethan nodded, his expression softening. "You're not alone, Lily. Whatever happens, we'll face it together."

Lily took a deep breath, the weight of their shared words sinking into her chest. She wasn't alone. She didn't have to do this by herself.

The figure nodded, their voice echoing in the stillness. "Then step forward. Step into the rift. And make your choice."

Lily's heart raced as she turned to face the darkness that lay ahead. The rift was waiting for her. She could feel it, like a pull in her chest, beckoning her to step forward.

And as she did, her mind was filled with a single, overwhelming thought: This is not the end.

www.ingramcontent.com/pod-product-compliance
Lightning Source LLC
LaVergne TN
LVHW010551070526
838199LV00063BA/4942